THE WEDLOCK CHRONICLES

THE WEDLOCK CHRONICLES

Volume 1

Donna M. N. Edwards

ISBN-13: 9781546726920
ISBN-10: 1546726926
Library of Congress Control Number: 2017908035
CreateSpace Independent Publishing Platform
North Charleston, South Carolina

This book is dedicated to
*My parents, Margaret and Montford D. Naylor, Jr., who
taught me the meaning of unconditional love;
my husband and best friend Keith, who has always been there for me;
and, to my children Nicole and Matthew, who I
pray find and keep their soul mates.*

Contents

Author's Notes

A year ago, I had no idea that I would be writing this book. Then our daughter got engaged. As we rejoiced in the couple's happiness, I vowed to be the best mother-in-law in the world and to give advice only when asked. With wedding preparations underway, I soon realized that they had made very little preparation for the real work that would start *after* the wedding. Marriage is so much more than a ring, a dress, and getting to the church on time. Most married couples pledge to love and be faithful forever regardless of finances, illness, and the like, but more often than we would prefer the marriages end in disappointment.

As a wife of more than thirty years, I recognized that even though my daughter and her fiancé had been spectators in their parents' marriages, and had agreed to attend pre-marriage counseling, other reality checks would also be helpful. Actual examples would go a long way in providing a more realistic view of what they would be facing. That's when I decided to share unsolicited advice from others.

I researched the marriages of twenty-five diverse, high-profile couples who remained committed to each other under stressful circumstances. While they represent the good, the bad, and the ugly parts of marriage, they are also examples of how perseverance and commitment can sustain a relationship. The "Notes" pages are provided for readers to write their reactions and/or questions regarding each section.

My findings led me on a complicated journey of self-reflection and created an awareness that the lessons contained in this book are universal.

Introduction

The "M" word. What is it about marriage that inspires reactions ranging from crying tears of joy to sobbing in despair? Regardless, while marriage is not for everyone, most of us take the leap of faith and marry anyway, hoping for the best. Statistics reveal that in the United States these matches made in heaven often lead to the opposite destination. But, there is hope. There are couples who have remained committed without having to be committed to any institution other than marriage.

This book highlights wedlock wisdom from a diverse group of people, married before the year 2000, who appear to have found some measure of marital success. In order to fully benefit from these insights, don't judge the messengers. Marriages are like fingerprints—all of them are different. People are not perfect and neither are marriages. All of us have done things that we regret. This book was written to give context to the struggles these couples overcame and the advice they shared, and to align the reader's expectations of marriage with the reality of marriage.

The challenges people face in marriages are common regardless of who they are or what type of work they do. While great respect and deference is given to all of the couples, they are referred to on a first name basis as a way of keeping the focus on their roles as husbands and wives.

These stories provide a keyhole view of these couples' lives from writings, individual quotes, and observations. No one really knows what goes on in a marriage except the wife, the husband, and God.

The Wedlock Chronicles, Volume I, is written in the form of fable-like vignettes with morals at the end of each story. This is intentionally in contrast to the fairy tale perceptions so often associated with marriage. These "marry-tales" are open invitations to everyone to learn from others' experiences and to re-think their preconceived ideas of marriage.

Ultimately, the most valuable lessons are not that the couples made mistakes or exhibited certain odd behaviors. The most important variables are communication, connection and commitment, and what part these factors played in strengthening their relationships. It is only by adopting this perspective that we will be able use their examples and advice in a way that will help us in our own lives. Now fasten your seat belts because the wedlock rollercoaster is a bumpy ride.

Donna E!/Depositphotos.com

Ken Todd and Lisa Vanderpump
Married: August 28, 1982

Ken Todd is a restauranteur and entrepreneur.
Lisa Vanderpump is a restauranteur and reality
star on "Real Housewives of Beverly Hills"
and "Vanderpump Rules."

Marriage: Keeping It Real

What began as Lisa pranking Todd, the owner of a pub she was visiting, culminated into a whirlwind marriage six weeks later. While he had never met her before, he was intrigued by her. Although she was 21 years old and Ken Todd, the owner was 37, she could hardly be called a gold digger. Lisa had gold of her own because she was a successful actress who had worked in the entertainment industry since she was nine.

What the two lacked in courtship time, they more than made up for in anniversaries. They have beaten the Hollywood odds and are still going strong after 34 years. The have a child of their own, Pandora, and an adopted son, Max. Lisa is stepmom to Ken's son Warren, five years her junior, who is the product of a previous marriage. Ken and Lisa own and operate a highly successful restaurant empire.

CHALLENGES
Their real-life drama is as follows:

- There is a sixteen-year age difference between the two.
- He's impulsive and she is more conservative.
- Lisa invited a houseguest to live with them and they eventually had to evict him.
- Their reality shows keep their relationship under the media's glare.
- Lisa had to adjust to a stepson who is five years her junior.

Through it all, they continue to grow with each other.

THE SECRETS OF THEIR SUCCESS

The sixteen-year gap in this couple's ages does not appear to be an issue. Ken and Lisa give new meaning to the adage "age ain't nothing but a number." They share the same goals and are intensely loyal to each other. They seem to always have each other's backs. For example, when they had to evict a houseguest Lisa had befriended, Ken fully supported her decision and was very protective of her.

While Ken is impulsive and Lisa is more conservative, Lisa sees this as a plus. She believes their skill sets complement each other and support their business and marital success. In business, this has led to them expanding their restaurant business. In their personal lives, they have renewed their vows at least twice and have been married for over three decades.

It is interesting that their marriage, while high profile and the subject of *two* reality shows, remains strong enough to withstand the media glare. This seems to be the exception and not the rule. A closer look at this formidable team may give some valuable insight. Ken and Lisa appear to be more adept at deciding *what parts of their reality they choose to share* with the world than their counterparts. So be it. It obviously works for them.

The Moral of This Story

Marriages are at their best when the husband and the wife demonstrate that they are on the same side.

ANONYMOUS

Notes

Kyra Sedgwick and Kevin Bacon
Married: September 4, 1988

Kyra Sedgwick is an American actress and producer.
Kevin Bacon is an American actor and musician.

Some Like It Hot

In the 1970s a shy, twelve-year-old girl had just enjoyed a matinee. Her brother encouraged her to compliment one of the actors she really liked. That actor was the then nineteen-year-old Kevin Bacon. In the 1980s Kyra met him again on a movie set. At that point, these two twenty somethings were co-starring in the film *Lemon Sky*. They began to date and it became serious. Then, one Christmas Eve it was Kevin's turn to be nervous. He had placed a ring in her stocking. When Kyra discovered it, he was on his knees and shaking. They married on September 4, 1988 and have maintained their personal co-star status ever since. The have two children—a son, Travis and a daughter, Sosie.

THE CHALLENGES
They have lived their fair share of drama, literally and figuratively.

- Early in their marriage, Kyra struggled with finding work.
- In 2008, they became victims of Bernie Madoff's Ponzi scheme. They lost their entire pension.
- Sometimes their work required them to be separated and there was difficulty balancing their relationship, family, and career.

Yet, they're still in the forefront of
sustained Hollywood marriages.

THE SECRETS OF THEIR SUCCESS
This couple seems to make it work with love, support, humor and a laser-like focus on their relationship. They firmly believe in giving their relationship top billing, before children and careers. They find time to be with each other and enjoy a healthy sex life. Kyra shared that she still finds

Kevin attractive and says that growing older with him is scary and exciting. She sees Kevin as a lover, helpmate, friend, father, and advisor. When Kyra struggled getting work, he helped her to understand that while she wasn't a megastar, her skill set would keep her in demand. Since Kyra has adopted that perspective, her career has remained on track.

In 2008, when they lost all of their pension money (most of which was Kevin's) in a Ponzi scheme, the couple passed the "for richer or poorer" test with flying colors. Kevin joked that when they first found out, they thought of having sex because at least that was free. Jokes aside, once they thought about it they realized that whatever happened, they had each other. Both kids were almost finished with school and they figured they could still work, so they just weathered the storm. Notice that they fought clean. They focused on addressing the issue *not* on assigning blame.

At one point, they discovered that they were distant cousins. For the show *Finding Your Roots*, a series in which famous Americans are given an insight into their family backgrounds, their DNA was tested. It was determined that they were 9th cousins and that Kevin shared common ancestors with Brad Pitt and President Obama. Kyra was initially concerned but Kevin assured her that as long as they weren't first cousins it did not matter.

Their marriage was tested again when they were forced to live on opposite coasts due to job assignments. Kevin stayed in New York with the children while she filmed *The Closer* in Los Angeles. While she missed some family events, Kyra made the most of her time with her family when she did see them. She believes that what keeps them strong is that they check in with each other regularly and Kevin definitely believes in having a sense of humor. His best advice? "Whatever you do, don't listen to celebrities on advice on how to stay married," Bacon teased. "That's my secret."

The Moral of This Story

Any marriage is hard work. But what I always say is,
"Keep the fights clean and the sex dirty."

KEVIN BACON

7

Notes

Bess and Harry Houdini
Married: June 22, 1894

Bess Houdini was the stage assistant and wife of Harry Houdini. Harry Houdini was a magician.

Spellbound

Bess and Harry were show business enthusiasts. Bess was Catholic and a singer/showgirl in the group *Floral Sisters*. Harry was a Jewish magician in the *Houdini Brothers* act. In 1894 in Coney Island, New York their paths crossed when Bess and her friend attended Harry's show. After the show, they met backstage and Harry was immediately under her spell. Shortly thereafter, he proposed and insisted they marry immediately.

According to Bess, she helped purchase her own ring and paid the cost of the marriage license. Three weeks later, they eloped in a civil ceremony. While Harry's mother was accepting of the pair, Bess' mother was not. Later, they would be married by a rabbi and yet again by a Catholic priest.

Initially, Harry and Bess were stage partners, but as he became more popular she transitioned to a more supportive role of designing costumes for his stage shows and managing his calendar. To Bess' disappointment, she could not have children but they did have a menagerie of birds, dogs, and cats.

THE CHALLENGES

While Bess and Harry had their own brand of magic, their relationship did experience some reality checks:

- Bess and Harry had an interfaith marriage. Harry was Jewish and Bess was a practicing Roman Catholic. Fortunately, Harry was not as devout.
- Harry had a brief three-month affair and was contrite.
- They could not have children but Harry was understanding about it.

- Harry was a total mama's boy. The relationship he had with his mother was legendary. He literally treated her like a queen and became inconsolable upon her death.

Still, they made magic.

THE SECRETS OF THEIR SUCCESS

Harry was a romantic, entertaining, and loving husband. During their marriage, Harry wooed Bess with love notes, flowers, jewelry, and over-the-top anniversary celebrations. The fact that Bess could not have children did not negatively affect their relationship. Harry's affections seemed already consumed with Bess and his mother, at the very least.

Bess was forgiving and calm. According to Harry, when they did have disagreements, she was so even tempered that their arguments were short lived. Bess was accepting and understanding of her husband's relationship with his mother, whom he doted on. The umbilical cord was severed only at the time of his mother's death—an event which left Harry emotionally paralyzed with grief. Bess even forgave a brief infidelity she knew of during his lifetime. Allegedly, soon after Harry's death, she found love letters written to her husband from other women. Ever the charming hostess, Bess invited all of them to tea and upon their departure gave them their letters as parting gifts.

Harry once characterized Bess as his soul mate and wrote in a love note to her that they "had starved together and starred together." Though there were some "smoke and mirrors" in their relationship, they weathered the storms and enjoyed the triumphs of matrimony. In spite of it all, they loved each other and remained committed to their relationship.

The Moral of This Story

Forgiveness is a virtue of the brave.

Indira Gandhi

Notes

Everett Collection Inc / Alamy Stock Photos

Frida Kahlo and Diego Rivera
Married: August 21, 1929; Divorced: November,
1939; Remarried: December 8, 1940

Frida Kahlo was a celebrated Mexican self-portraitist, surrealist, and political activist.
Diego Rivera was a celebrated Mexican muralist.

Feeling the Burn

In 1922, a very young Frida briefly encountered Diego as he was painting a mural at her school. She would not see him again for several years. In 1925, Frida was injured in a bus accident, which required her to have various surgeries throughout her life. After a long recovery period, she attended a friend's party in the late 1920's and was formally introduced to Diego. Frida asked him to look at her art to determine if she had potential. He was impressed with her work and told her so. Though he had two common-law wives and was a self-confessed serial cheater, they began to date. On August 21, 1929, the 42-year-old, six foot, three-hundred pound Diego married the 22-year-old, five-foot-three, ninety pound Frida.

THE CHALLENGES

While they looked different, they were both well-respected artists whose temperaments were quite similar. He was fire and she was gasoline and so the relationship was always not only hot, but explosive. Both of them cheated. Frida cheated with both men and women. Diego was accepting of the women but not of the men. Diego actually had an affair with Frida's younger sister which caused Frida to become completely incensed. At one point, Diego contemplated asking his doctor for a note that would explain that it was impossible for him to be faithful.

Other issues:

- Frida was devastated that she could not have children due to injuries from the 1925 bus accident.
- Frida was often in pain as a result of those injuries.

*They divorced in November of 1939, only
to remarry on December 8, 1940.
They resorted to the same behaviors.*

THE SECRETS OF THEIR SUCCESS

Their living arrangements were usually separate but nearby each other. For example, they built a house that had two separate residences placed on opposite sides of a bridge. It almost seemed like a metaphor for their relationship. They could not live with each other but they could not live without each other.

They deeply admired each other's talents and supported each other. Even during their one year of divorce, they remained friendly and Frida helped Diego with his finances and correspondence. The fact that they remarried while their behaviors did not change, and they remained married, strongly suggests that there was a tacit agreement to accept the relationship as it was.

Frida explained what he meant to her when she said that Diego was "her everything; her child, her lover, her universe." Yet, she understood his limitations as she observed that, "I cannot speak of Diego as my husband because that term, when applied to him, is an absurdity. He never has been, nor will he ever be, anybody's husband."

Upon her death, Diego lamented that he realized too late that the best part of his life was when he loved her. In later years when he was married to someone else, he asked that when he died his ashes be united with Frida. They never were. While their marriage wasn't picture perfect it was uniquely beautiful to them.

The Moral of the Story

Commitment is making a choice to give up other choices.

Scott Stanley

Notes

DonnaE!/Depositphotos.com
Barack and Michelle Obama
Married: October 3, 1992

*Barack Obama, the 44th President of the United States
of America, is a lawyer and published author.
Michelle Obama, an American lawyer and writer,
served as first lady from 2009-2017.*

West Wing Wisdom

This couple's relationship is compelling because their three-year court-ship was a foreshadowing, a virtual dress rehearsal of their marriage. The parallels between their courtship and marriage are striking:

- When they first met on the job, Michelle was assigned as Barack's advisor–a role she would often assume during their marriage.
- During their courtship, Barack returned to Harvard and they had to navigate a long-distance relationship. Once married, they had to endure periods of separation when he wrote a book and ran for public office.
- Michelle knew that Barack was not rich (the car he was driving had a hole in it). True to form, during their marriage Michelle was torn about becoming a working mom but was pragmatic about their financial circumstances.
- They leaned on each other during times of hardship. When Michelle's dad died unexpectedly, Barack left school to be by her side. Once married, she had to support him when his mother and grandmother died.
- They celebrated Barack being the first African American president of the Harvard Law Review and post-wedding, celebrated his election as the first acknowledged African American President of the United States.

Moreover, this couple experienced sharing their honest opinions with one another. They frequently had lively debates, including ones about the insti-tution of marriage. Michelle was a proponent of marriage, while Barack wondered aloud if it was even necessary. The two vigorously discussed the matter one evening at a posh Chicago restaurant. Barack ended the fili-buster and her commentary by presenting her with an engagement ring. That drop-the-mic moment would mirror some of his future performances in their personal and public lives.

While it appears that they were able to "test drive" the relationship before marriage, just like every other couple, after the wedding, tune ups are still necessary.

CHALLENGES

- Michelle felt that they needed to put themselves higher on their 'to do' list.
- Barack was accustomed to periods of separation because he had experienced it with his mother. Michelle preferred a closer-knit family.
- Barack enjoyed politics, while Michelle did not.
- Michelle struggled with her decision to be a working mom.

*Through it all, they continue to give their
marriage the VIP treatment.*

THE SECRETS OF THEIR SUCCESS

Michelle and Barack give credit to each other for the success of their mar-riage. Michelle acknowledges that she is "fortunate ... to have a husband who loves me and shows me in every way." She admits she was attracted to "… his emotional honesty… There are no games with him—he is who he appears to be." Barack is adamant that without Michelle he would not have gotten where he is today. He says that she is both brilliant and beau-tiful. Their love, respect, and admiration for each other is evident.

As for their challenges, they are quick to admit that their marriage is not perfect. They struggled with Barack's extended absences from the home. Michelle said she had to accept that she was not going to have a conventional marriage and that her husband would be away a lot. During long absences, they always talked at least twice a day. She also decided to become a working mom and she got great support from her mom.

While Barack wanted a political life, Michelle was not immediately taken with being a political wife. Michelle's compromise was to support him as he needed it. Ironically, his presidential win was a personal win for the couple. Michelle marvelled that "it was the first time in years they had lived seven days a week in the same household with the same schedule, with the same set of rituals." They began to put themselves a little higher on the 'to do' list by engaging in activities such as exercising together, seeing the kids off to school and going on dates together - no matter how tired they were.

If approval ratings are any indication, Michelle grew into the role of political wife quite well. There are also indications that she revealed attributes Barack had not seen before. He remarked "... it's [the] tension between familiarity and mystery that makes for something strong, because, even as you build a life of ... mutual support, you retain some sense of surprise or wonder about the other person."

Both parties insist that a good marriage takes hard work. Michelle emphasizes that the equality of a marriage should be measured over the life of the marriage. Excellent advice.

The Moral of This Story

You have to do the work in your marriage, but it has to be laid on a strong foundation of love.

ROBIN WRIGHT

Notes

Keystone Pictures USA / Alamy Stock Photos

Clementine and Winston Churchill
Married: September 12, 1908

*Clementine Churchill was the wife and
advisor of Winston Churchill.
Winston Churchill was the Prime Minister of England
during World War II, a writer, and a Nobel Peace Prize
recipient. He was also married with children.*

Keep Calm and Stay Married

In his public life, Winston Churchill was known for his gruff, strong exterior but in his personal life, he had met his match in Clementine. He first met her in 1904. He didn't see her again until 1908 when he was seated next to her at a dinner party. There was an instant attraction. He was taken with her beauty, intelligence, liveliness, and the fact that she was actually interested in what he had to say. Clementine, who said she would have been in politics if she had been a man, enjoyed hearing about political events as seen through the eyes of an up-and-coming politician. By September 12, 1908, the same year women were fighting for the right to vote in England, they married. They subsequently had five children.

THE CHALLENGES

Winston travelled frequently which caused them to be apart at times. Clementine had a fiery personality and, in private, was not afraid to loudly and skillfully challenge Winston.

Other stressors on the relationship:

- Winston was Prime Minister of England during World War II when their country was being bombed. While not his words, the World War II slogan "Keep Calm and Carry On" described the attitude and spirit of his leadership.
- They lost one child at age three due to illness and another daughter committed suicide.

They remained married until Winston's death.

THE SECRETS OF THEIR SUCCESS

Clementine knew that in the beginning of their marriage some people thought that she was not a good match for Winston. She made it her mission to prove them wrong. She became his confidante, she reviewed his speeches, comforted him when he lost elections and became his "go to" person in times of crises. Their skill sets complemented each other. In public, Winston was blunt and had a biting wit, while Clementine was more charming and diplomatic. This worked well because when he "ruffled feathers" her charming approach would ensure that all was forgiven.

While Clementine was charming with others, when she corrected Winston outside of public view she was not. As years passed, she learned how to express her opinions in a kinder way. Regardless of what she said or how she said it, clearly Winston was her priority. Their daughter Mary once remarked that, "Daddy comes first, second and third."

For his part, Winston was the peacemaker in the relationship. If they disagreed, he tried to appease Clementine. He once commented "if you are going through hell, keep going." Regardless of the circumstances, both parties were totally committed to the relationship. They were in it to win it and they faced adversity with a united and determined front.

The Moral of This Story

Lean on each other's strengths and forgive each other's weaknesses.

ANONYMOUS

Notes

DonnaE!/Donnie Simpson on twitter

Donnie and Pam Simpson
Married: October 13, 1973

*Donnie Simpson is an American radio DJ as well
as a television and movie personality
in Washington, D.C.
Pam Simpson is a housewife and former model and actress.*

A Love Remix

The backdrop for this relationship should be set to music. Donnie's father owned a record shop and so it was only natural that his world would come alive with the sound of music. This led to Donnie's first DJ job at the age of 15. About a year later, a strikingly beautiful fellow high school student named Pam caught Donnie's eye. Neither Pam nor Donnie knew then how these two events would lead them on a love journey of friendship, fame, fortune, and forgiveness. The pair dated for over two years. Then one sunny afternoon on October 13, 1973, these two nineteen-year-old natives of Detroit married. Donnie continued to work as a DJ in Detroit for about four more years until the couple relocated to Washington, D.C., where he pursued a job at WKYS. With Pam's unfettered love and support and his talent, Donnie's career skyrocketed. They enjoyed wealth and fame and were blessed with two children—a boy and a girl.

What happened between the "I Do" and the "happily ever after" is ordinary, instructive, and heart warming.

THE CHALLENGES

On paper, this couple was perfect. They had all the trappings—cute girl, good looking guy, high school sweethearts, similar backgrounds, supportive family, and two adorable children. But behind the veneer of "having it all," this couple was human and their soundtrack was not always on track:

- Over time the pair communicated less frequently and not as well.
- The two took each other for granted.
- At one point, their household revolved mostly around Donnie.

- After 19 years of marriage, Donnie left his wife and children for a younger woman for about three years.

Notwithstanding the discord, they are now in harmony.

THE SECRETS OF THEIR SUCCESS

This couple are the quintessential "comeback kids" and their comeback is remarkable in a world where troubled relationships almost always end in divorce. During Donnie's three-year hiatus from his family, Pam tried to save the marriage and they went to counseling. Unfortunately, at that time, Donnie was not receptive. Formal separation papers were prepared. This is where this story differs from most. Since there were no money issues during the separation, neither pursued a divorce. Even though their relationship was awkward, they were polite and still cared for each other.

Donnie remained rudderless and had no idea how to regain his emotional balance. Pam angrily tried to parent their two teenagers alone and sought individual counseling. The counseling helped her focus on herself and their children. It helped her to realize that she and Donnie were both struggling and that while she was hurt, she did not want to hurt him. Pam also knew that for their marriage survive, changes would have to be made.

Eventually, an emotionally exhausted and humbled Donnie also engaged in individual counseling and decided he wanted to reconnect with Pam. For six months, the couple considered the terms of a possible reconciliation. They discussed the non-negotiables and accountability. The process of rebuilding trust, forgiving, and making changes was not easy, but it was necessary. They have reunited and are honest about what is needed to achieve successful reconciliation. Pam cautions that you may have to swallow your pride, but hold on to your self-respect. Donnie recommends that if you still have feelings for your spouse, do everything you can to keep your relationship intact.

The Moral of This Story

It is better to lose your pride with someone you love rather than to lose that someone you love with your useless pride.

JOHN RUSKIN

Notes

DonnaE!/Library of Congress online

Jack and Jackie Kennedy
Married: September 12, 1953

John F. Kennedy (Jack) was the 35th President of the United States and was assassinated on November 22, 1963. Jacqueline Bouvier Kennedy (Jackie) served as first lady from 1961 to 1963 and was a book editor.

Who's Your Daddy?

Though Jack was twelve years Jackie's senior, they had similar backgrounds. They both came from wealthy, Catholic families. They were well-educated and well-traveled. They even socialized in the same circles. He wanted to be President one day and Jackie longed for an unpredictable life. The couple was formally introduced in 1952 at a dinner party. She was engaged to a stockbroker at the time but she and the future president "clicked." Shortly after that dinner party, Jackie ended her engagement and began dating Jack. It is noteworthy that Jackie knew that he was a playboy and was aware that his father, Joe, was a serial cheater. Her father Black Jack Bouvier also liked the ladies (which in part caused the divorce from her mother), so she was well-acquainted with this behavior.

While Jack was a confirmed bachelor, his father, Joe Kennedy encouraged him to marry because it would help his political career. Joe explained that he did not have to give up his "extracurricular activities"—just marry a woman who would be an asset to him as he pursued his political aspirations. In 1953, Jack proposed and Jackie accepted. They were married in September of that year.

He admired his father and she admired hers. Given that their fathers had similar attitudes and behavioral patterns, it seemed like a perfect match, right? Not necessarily … as in all relationships, the devil is in the details.

THE CHALLENGES

While Jackie knew that Jack was a notorious womanizer, she thought she could handle it because "all men behave that way." It was his refusal to be discreet that infuriated her. While he had not been discreet before they married, it appeared that she thought a marriage certificate would change all of that. Jackie apparently saw no connection with his behavior and that of his father (who once went on a cruise with his wife and paid for his mistress to occupy a separate cabin). It was rumored that Jackie was so humiliated by Jack's flagrant bedhopping that she retaliated by having affairs of her own. Allegedly, she also wanted a divorce but Joe Kennedy offered her one million dollars to stay.

Other stressors on the relationship included:

- Jack had a bad back and was in constant pain. Back problems nearly led to his death on one or more occasions.
- They had five children but three died (a still birth, a death of a child shortly after a birth and a miscarriage).
- The country was divided about Civil Rights issues and death threats were made against Jack.

Nonetheless, they remained married until Jack's assassination in November of 1963.

THE SECRETS OF THEIR SUCCESS
The Obvious
Jackie was the total package as a political wife. She always looked stunning. In addition, she spoke several languages, was charming, and was an astute judge of character. Jack was handsome, charismatic, intellectually curious, and had a great sense of humor. She loved her lifestyle with him and he loved that her value added to his agenda.

The Real Deal
They loved each other at their worst as well as when they were at their best. Ironically, tragedy and stress—of which there was no shortage in their lives—strengthened the relationship. When their last baby clung to life and eventually died, Jack had the television in Mrs. Kennedy's room disabled so that he could temper the bad news. When Jack was being shot to death as they rode through Dallas, Texas, Jackie did not duck. She

climbed onto the back of that car to retrieve pieces of Jack's skull in the hopes that he could be put back together again. Her first instinct was not of self-preservation, it was to help him. Their relationship was not perfect, but it was theirs.

The Moral of This Story

Love me when I least deserve it because that is when I really need it.

SWEDISH PROVERB

Notes

DonnaE!/Depositphotos.com

James Garner and Lois Clarke Garner
Married: August 17, 1956

James Garner was an actor, producer, and voice artist.
Lois Clarke Garner is a widow and homemaker.

Sticking to the Script

James Garner and Lois Clarke Garner have a story that could have been played out on an MGM movie set. They met at a political rally and went out every night after that for two weeks. James says it was love at first sight.

Lois remembers it a bit differently. She says they met a week before the rally at a barbeque. She claims he flew into the backyard and asked permission to swim in the pool as he dove into the water.

What they both remembered is that they were so taken with each other that two weeks after the rally, they married at the Beverly Hills Court House. They enjoyed a $77 honeymoon (a princely sum at that time). After they married, he adopted his wife's daughter and the next year they were blessed with their own daughter.

THE CHALLENGES
This couple did experience some undesired script changes:

- While their marriage did not become a casualty of his rumored affairs with various Hollywood actresses, it did suffer some injuries.
- During what might be described as a midlife crisis, James lived away from the home for about eighteen months. Lois' girlfriends suggested she kick him off the set. She did not.
- Lois had a handicapped daughter.
- His parents thought they had little in common. Lois was Jewish, a dreamer, preferred to stay indoors and was from Los Angeles. James was practical, an outdoors type, Methodist and from a small town in Oklahoma.

Still, this couple starred in a personal blockbuster movie that ended as a classic.

THE SECRET OF THEIR SUCCESS

While they had little in common, James saw their differences as strengths. It was his belief that they balanced each other. Neither one of them were particularly religious, so there was really no conflict with religion.

Lois saw James as her hero or at least appreciated his acceptance of her and her baggage. She admitted that she was "an emotional wreck" when she met him and at that time her daughter was suffering from polio. He not only married Lois, he adopted her sick child. It is not a stretch to say that she may have felt compelled to return the favor and accept his baggage when he was experiencing a melt down that some might characterize as male "mental-pause".

Ultimately, he and Lois were the co-stars in their marriage and everyone else fell into the category of supporting cast members or extras. This couple knew what they felt for each other and what they were willing to sacrifice for their relationship. In the end, they stayed married for almost 48 years until James' death. Kudos to them!

The Moral of This Story

The success of marriage comes not in finding the "right" person, but in the ability of both partners to adjust to the real person they inevitably realize they married.

JOHN FISCHER

Notes

WENN Ltd/Alamy Stock Photo
Alma and Colin Powell
Married: August 25, 1962

*Alma was an audiologist, radio show host, and is currently
Chair of America's Promise and a published author.
Colin who once served as the National Security Advisor,
Chairman of the Joint Chiefs of Staff and Secretary of
State, is a public speaker, and published author.*

When Love Begins Blind

In 1961, an army friend asked Colin Powell to go on a blind date with his girlfriend's roommate. Colin agreed against his own instincts. The girlfriend asked Alma to take the same leap of faith. Alma was less enthusiastic about the opportunity than Colin. The evening exceeded both their expectations. He was mesmerized by her green eyes. She thought he was the nicest person she ever met.

They dated for eight months and then he got his military orders. In a matter of months, he would be deployed to Vietnam. Colin asked her to write him. Alma told him their relationship was over. He came back the next day and, without a ring, proposed. He explained that the money for the ring could be better spent on household items. Alma accepted and told him that "he could make it up to her later." Two weeks later, these risk takers exchanged plain gold bands and marched down a church aisle into "ever after."

FYI: True to his word, he did eventually get her a "rock."

THE CHALLENGES

A military family's lifestyle is not an easy one. The travel may look glamorous but constant travel can be wearing. They moved over eighteen times. Other stressors on the relationship:

- Deployment was difficult. Colin described his feelings about being away from his family in his book *My American Journey*: "I felt a confusion of emotions on leaving the house at Dale City, loss at missing out on the beautiful moments in my children's growing-up, a touch of guilt at not bearing my share of the responsibility, and even a twinge of regret that they all seemed to be doing fine without me."

- Alma suffered from depression.
- There were rumors of Colin's infidelity.
- There was political pressure for Colin to run for President, but Alma was steadfastly opposed to it.

Nonetheless, their marriage remains
"front and center" in their lives.

THE SECRETS OF THEIR SUCCESS

Alma characterizes their marriage as one that is based on mutual trust and respect and it is significant that these building blocks were established *before* their marriage. When they were dating and Colin was comfortable deploying without making a commitment, she announced that the relationship was over because she knew her worth. Once he had a night to think about it, so did he. He later said: "Alma had everything I would ever want in a wife. I was a jerk for not acting before she got away. This nonsense that if the Army wanted you to have a wife it would have issued you one had to go. . ." He could not get her ring immediately but she knew that was not essential to their relationship. What was most important to Alma was that she be honored with a commitment and that they work together as a team. He received her message as he later said, ". . . She was wise enough to know that the trappings tell little about success in marriage." Colin also saw that she could defer immediate gratification for greater priorities. For a man with a military career, this attribute is particularly important in a mate.

By all appearances, they remain devoted to one another. While Colin is the front man in the relationship, he has always seen Alma as his foundation. He describes his wedding day as his luckiest day. Alma maintains that they support one another in any undertaking. This is borne out in their actions. Though deployment was difficult, Colin always came home and Alma was there for him. When Alma was recovering from depression, Colin stood by her. When Colin had to address allegations of his infidelity, Alma stood by him. When they had to withstand political pressure for

Colin to run for President, they made a decision that they could *both* live with. After over a half century of marriage, this classy couple is a shining example of love, faith, and dignity.

The Moral of This Story

Personal worth is not negotiable and commitments, not promises, sustain a relationship.

DONNA M. N. EDWARDS

Notes

DonnaE!/ Internet, Photographer unknown
Paul and Julia Child
Married: September 1, 1946

Paul Child was involved in espionage and was a diplomat.
Julia Child was involved in espionage and was a master chef.

When You Find Romance on Your Menu

This odd couple were best friends forever before they began their foray into romance. Paul and Julia were frequent dinner partners and worked with spies. They both loved exotic foods and thrived in dangerous situations (she processed top secret communications and he designed war rooms for generals). That, however, was where the similarities ended. Five-foot-ten Paul was a worldly 42-year-old man who enjoyed wine, sex, art, and photography. Six-foot-two Julia was a 32-year-old classy, naïve virgin with a crazy sense of humor. At that time, her age made her an old maid—a woman who was past her prime in terms of marriage.

That notwithstanding, sometime during the end of World War II, this pair of "foodies" breathed new life into the lyrics "It's heaven when you, find romance on your menu." When the war finally ended, their marriage began on September 1, 1946 in Washington, D.C. They did not have a honeymoon, however, in 1948, the State Department sent Paul on a diplomatic posting to Paris for two years. This provided the perfect backdrop for Julia, who loved to cook for Paul, to master French cuisine. Then—voila—she became a star!

THE CHALLENGES
Life was not a bowl of cherries for them. Here were some of the pitfalls:

- The day before their wedding they had a car accident.
- Julia was disappointed that she could not have children.
- She did not get along with some members of his family.

Still, they could withstand the heat, so
they "stayed in the kitchen."

THE SECRETS OF THEIR SUCCESS

Overall their relationship worked because they worked at it. Julia explained that their marriage was happy because, "We are a team. We were friends as well as husband and wife. We just have a good time." Paul agreed saying that, "We are never not together." Their lusty love letters indicate that was the case in more ways than one. It was as though they were on a perpetual date.

That is not to say they did not have bumps in the road, so to speak. Their injuries from their "wedding eve" car accident were minimal. While Julia was concerned that she couldn't have children, Paul was fine without them. Sometimes Julia found it difficult to get along with a couple of his family members but that was easily remedied by limiting her time with them.

It is interesting that in the beginning of their marriage, Julia followed Paul whenever and wherever the State Department sent him and she supported him in his work. Once he retired, he became her support system and her number one fan. This was unusual for men of his era. He was definitely a man ahead of his time, but on time for their marriage. He once said, "Without Julia, I think I'd be a sour old bastard living off in a cave." Julia expressed that she owed her success to Paul. Both were eager to point out the other's attributes. A true sign of a loving relationship.

The Moral of This Story

Date your mate.

ANONYMOUS

Notes

Granamour Weems Collection / Alamy Stock Photos

Nickolas Ashford and Valerie Simpson
Married: November 30, 1974

Nick Ashford and Valerie Simpson were American R&B singers and songwriters who formed the musical partnership Ashford & Simpson. Nick Ashford is now deceased and Valerie Simpson is still working.

Music to Their Ears

While it wasn't love at first sight for Nick and Valerie, they discovered in record time that song writing was music to their ears. In 1964, twenty-one-year old Nick and seventeen-year-old Valerie met in a Harlem church where they sang in the choir. It wasn't long before they began writing and publishing gospel songs. The pair eventually expanded their reach to secular songs.

On a personal level, Nick initially thought Valerie was too young for him, so they just remained good friends who just worked together. Valerie said she thought she tried too hard and that scared him off. At any rate, they both dated other people and when people would ask Valerie why they weren't together she would say, "He's like a brother to me." It was only after they became a couple that Nick confessed to her that it irked him when she made that remark. They shared a platonic working partnership for about eight years. After an extended period of friendship, they lived together for two years. Valerie became pregnant and they bought a house. Shortly after that Nick and Valerie married.

THE CHALLENGES
Though they generally worked and lived well together, they were not always on the same sheet of music:

- They disagreed on certain chords and had to rewrite the same song several times.
- They sometimes argued loudly and publicly. At one point, Nick felt that when they argued the relationship might be over.
- Nick felt they should not take vacations between ages of 25 and 40. Valerie did not agree.

Throughout all of this, their relationship remained noteworthy.

THE SECRETS OF THEIR SUCCESS

Valerie and Nick agreed that to have a successful marriage you must keep talking, laughing, and having as much sex as possible. Nick enjoyed being married because he could share his deepest thoughts and emotions with his best friend. He said that Valerie taught him that they could make up and make love as many times as they fought.

Valerie felt that what strengthened their relationship were the eight years that they got to know each other as friends and business partners. There was no pretense involved when they became a couple because they already knew each other. Even though they were always together, Valerie never felt stifled and, now since Nick's death, she misses his companionship.

True to their partnership, the couple had written a song about the success of their marriage. It is entitled "Solid," and it will forever be remembered as their anthem.

The Moral of This Story

Fighting doesn't mean there is something wrong, it means that something is surfacing that needs attention.

DR. JUDITH WRIGHT

Notes

DonnaE!/Depositphotos.com
Phillip and Robin McGraw
Married: August 14, 1976

*Phillip McGraw (Dr. Phil) is a daytime talk
show host, psychologist, and author.
Robin McGraw is a women's advocate and #1
New York Times best-selling author.*

Marriage: "How's That Working for You?"

If you have ever watched the *Dr. Phil Show*, you may have heard him challenge a guest by asking, "So, how's that working for you?" Invariably, the person is forced to admit that things could be better, otherwise why would they be seeking his help?

Not long ago, it was rumored Phillip's marriage was in jeopardy, which made some wonder how he and his wife would answer that question. Before sharing their response, it is important to understand the context of their relationship.

Brenda, Phillip's sister and Robin were friends. Brenda invited Robin to their home where Robin met Phillip. He had been briefly married before (the relationship was annulled) and was home from school where he was studying to be a psychologist. Brenda and Robin went to her room to talk, but were unaware that a vent in Phillip's room allowed him to hear their entire conversation - including Robin's admiration of him.

They dated for three years even though very early courtship Robin made it clear that she wanted a meaningful relationship that would result in marriage. Then Robin told Phillip that she was ready for marriage and he explained that he was not. They broke up but talked on the phone every day for three weeks. Phillip re-evaluated his position and, after graduating, instead of attending his commencement exercises, he married Robin. They have two children and have never looked back.

THE CHALLENGES

Every marriage has its ups and downs. The couple agrees that they have endured the normal "speed bumps" in marriage such as scheduling issues and parenting. Other challenges include:

- They both carried the baggage of living in homes with alcoholic fathers. This common experience made the two of them closer and more determined that their children not grow up in a home with an alcoholic parent.
- Robin shows her emotions. Phillip does not show his emotions as much.
- Their relationship was attacked and mischaracterized in the media.

And yet this couple insists that they are happily married.

THE SECRETS OF THEIR SUCCESS

According to Robin, there is no secret to their marital success. They did their homework during their courtship and before the big entrance exam – marriage. Phillip and Robin first discussed what they needed from a marriage. Phillip says they spent three years working out their problems *before* the wedding. They also decided how they would resolve problems that might arise in the future. For example, they decided it was better to work out smaller problems before they became big issues. Once they settled on a game plan, they lived by it.

While the goal of some couples is to stay married, Phillip and Robin have been intentional about their goal of staying *happily* married. Robin says they learn each other's needs and are still focused on that. The conversation about their needs is fluid, as needs can change over time.

While Phillip does agree that living and working together may not be ideal for every couple, it has worked for them. They find that sharing their perspectives of their common experiences throughout the day is enjoyable and keeps them connected.

A key factor in the success of their marriage is that Phillip and Robin have made their relationship their top priority and have kept it very personal. Friends, media, and family members, no matter how well intentioned, are not invited into their relationship.

Though their 40-plus years' relationship is strictly private, their approach to maintaining it is not. Phillip shared their strategies in a book entitled, "Relationship Rescue: A Seven-Step Strategy for Reconnecting with Your Partner." What better way to answer the question, "How's that working for you?"

The Moral of This Story

Long-lasting love doesn't happen by accident... Love is deliberate, it's intentional, it's purposeful, and in the end, it's worth every minute that we give of ourselves to another.

DARLENE SCHACHT

Notes

Emilio and Gloria Estefan
Married: September 2, 1978

Emilio Estefan is a Cuban-American musician and producer who has won 19 Grammy Awards. Gloria Estefan is a Cuban-American singer, songwriter, actress, and businesswoman.

Making Beautiful Music Together

When a mutual friend asked Emilio to give Gloria and some friends advice about starting a band, the couple had no idea that the conversation would lead to a lifetime collaboration. At the time, the hardworking Emilio had two jobs. He was a sales manager for Bacardi, a leading producer of rum, and a keyboardist for the *Miami Latin Boys*, a band which played popular Latin music. He had heard Gloria sing and was impressed, and when he saw her at a wedding where his band was playing, he asked her to sit in. Shortly after that, he asked her to perform as lead singer with the band and though she was very shy, she agreed.

Gloria was pursuing a degree in Psychology at the University of Miami and initially sang with the band just on the weekends. Eventually, Emilio encouraged Gloria to overcome her shyness. After she had been in the group about eighteen months, the group changed its name to the *Miami Sound Machine* and began making recordings. That was not all that changed. What had begun as a professional relationship for Emilio and Gloria had become personal and on September 2, 1978, they were married. Their son Nayib was born two years later, on their anniversary. Their daughter Emily was born in March of 1994.

THE CHALLENGES

The Estefan's relationship was not without trials and tribulations. There were minor business-related lawsuits. There were also times when the family was not together because Gloria had to tour. Additionally:

- In March 1990, their tour bus was rear ended by a tractor trailer during a storm. Nayib, their son, had a fractured shoulder and Emilio had minor head and hand injuries. Gloria sustained serious injuries and had a long recovery period.

- They wanted another child and Gloria had difficulty conceiving after her accident.
- In 1995, in a boating accident, their vessel was hit by another boat. Though they were cleared of any wrongdoing, a twenty-nine-year-old law student died in that incident. This deeply affected the couple.
- In 2001 and 2002, they were stalked and harassed by a Venezuelan actor and had to take legal action to address the situation.

Yet, they have not missed a beat.

THE SECRETS OF THEIR SUCCESS

Emilio jokes that to be successful as a couple the man should say "yes" to everything the woman says. On a more serious note, he shares that they were both poor Cuban immigrants who worked hard and wanted to set an example for future generations.

Gloria admires Emilio because he is motivating and wakes up every day in a good mood. She says that he could have been a professional comedian and that he always makes her laugh. Gloria acknowledges the challenges in their lives but says that problems like the bus accident can either tear you apart or make you stronger. She is grateful that their problems made them a more tight-knit family. While Gloria does not advocate that all couples work together, she explained why it works for them when she said, "We just happen to get along. We're different, so we balance each other out. But our values and priorities are the same and we rarely differ on business decisions. We have the same goals and our family's always number 1."

The Moral of This Story

A good relationship requires two people who balance each other and are always there for one another.

ANONYMOUS

Notes

DonnaE!/BettmanCORBIS Photos

Doria Palmieri and Ron Prescott Reagan
Married: November 24, 1980

Doria Palmieri was a psychologist.
Ron Reagan is a radio talk show host, author,
and political analyst. He is also
President Reagan's son.

Dancing with a Star

I n 1977, at a dance studio, their eyes met first and their feet followed. Though Ron Reagan was seven years her junior, Doria Palmieri, a psychologist, continued to date him for the next 3 years, even though his parents did not approve. They were not sure her intentions were sincere. Ron, consistent with his rebel-with-a-cause spirit, neither needed nor sought their approval.

Then, in 1980, the unimaginable happened—his father ran for public office and won! Twenty days later, Ron and Doria quietly entered a judge's chamber to obtain a marriage license. The judge recommended that they get married immediately to avoid the paparazzi. Though they acted on the recommendation it was too late. While the only witness to the ceremony was the Secret Service person assigned to them, when they left the chambers there were a hoard of other witnesses—with cameras and questions. Apparently, someone leaked their whereabouts to the press. President-elect Ronald Reagan and First Lady-to-Be Nancy Reagan were none too pleased but were powerless to alter the outcome.

Over time, attitudes toward Doria did improve. Ron and Doria went on to enjoy a lasting, loving relationship. Though the two never had children, they "co-parented" three cats.

Sadly, in 2014, their union was involuntarily and permanently interrupted by Doria's death from natural causes.

THE CHALLENGES
Here's what went on in their Situation Room:

- The most obvious issue they faced was the "fish bowl" affect of Ron's father's presidency. The couple was constantly under the media glare.
- They had to endure false rumors about Ron's sexuality.
- His parents, the uninvited guests to their wedding, had to warm up to their daughter-in-law.
- Then there were the normal couple-type concerns (i.e., one obvious concern was their modest income. Once he was only making $11,000 as a ballet dancer. At another point, she was working and he had lost his job at the radio station as it went bankrupt. They had lost their health care and weren't sure what they should do.)

Throughout all of this, their relationship flourished for a full term.

THE SECRETS OF THEIR SUCCESS

It is important to note that "for better or for worse" this relationship survived two Reagan terms. Ron and Doria passed the for richer or poorer clause (they stayed together during the lean years) as well as the "in sickness and in health" clause (when Doria's health declined, Ron stayed by her side). This couple demonstrated their commitment to their marriage and their love for one another against all odds.

When it was suggested that Ron might have married for political reasons, he scoffed, "Why else do two people get married except that they love each other and want to?" It seemed as though controversy fueled their determination. They had a vision of their lives together and they never lost sight of it.

The Moral of This Story

A good marriage is worth fighting for.

LISA JACOBSON

Notes

Donna E!/Unknown photographer

Marie and Pierre Curie
Married: July 26, 1895

Marie and Pierre Curie along with another scientist, Henri Becquerel, won the Nobel Peace Prize for their work on radiation. Marie received a second Nobel Peace Prize for Chemistry.

Great Chemistry

While at the Sorbonne in Paris, Marie was introduced to Pierre by one of their professors. She found him attractive and smart. He was smitten with her and shared her passion for science. Simply put, they enjoyed great chemistry on every level. Within a year, Pierre proposed to her but she refused because she planned on returning to her native Poland to work. As fate would have it, the Krakow University would not accept Marie based upon her gender. He begged Marie to return to France where she could work at the Sorbonne. On July 26, 1895, they got married in Sceaux. In lieu of a wedding dress, the practical Marie wore a dark blue dress that she could wear in the lab. For their honeymoon, they engaged in one of their favorite past times by cycling across the French countryside.

At Marie's encouragement, Pierre completed his doctorate. They continued their scientific research on radiation with Henri Becquerel. This culminated in a nomination for a Nobel Peace Prize. In addition, they had two daughters.

THE CHALLENGES
While it would seem that this couple enjoyed a near perfect life, they had their struggles:

- Though Pierre encouraged her to get her doctorate, it was difficult for Marie to balance her work and parental duties with their daughters.
- She defied convention by working in a scientific field that, at that time, was dominated solely by men. Accordingly, when their work

was nominated for the Nobel Peace Prize, Marie's name was not even included.

Throughout all of this, they not only survived, they thrived.

THE SECRETS OF THEIR SUCCESS

This couple had a deep respect for each other's work ethic and intellect. They supported each other in every aspect of their relationship. While Marie was working to complete her doctorate, Pierre's father came to live with the couple to help raise the children. When Pierre discovered that her name had been omitted from the nomination, he lobbied on her behalf until it was included. Marie then became the first woman to be awarded the Nobel Peace Prize. Pierre truly saw Marie as his partner and as an equal, and he was adamant that others viewed her that way as well. Their mutual respect and admiration for each other made for a dynamic and very successful pairing.

Marie said of Pierre:
"Pierre Curie came to see me and showed a simple and sincere sympathy with my student life. Soon he caught the habit of speaking to me of his dream of an existence consecrated entirely to scientific research, and he asked me to share that life."

Pierre said of Marie:
"It would be a fine thing, in which I hardly dare believe, to pass our lives near each other, hypnotized by our dreams."

One can only imagine how difficult it must have been for Marie when Pierre died in an accident in 1906. She went on to be awarded a second Nobel Peace Prize and dedicated the rest of her life to working in his memory.

The Moral of This Story

Love is a partnership of two unique people who bring out the very best in each other, and who know that even though they are wonderful as individuals, they are even better together.

BARBARA CAGE

Notes

Maury Povich and Connie Chung
Married: December 2, 1984

Maury Povich is a talk show host.
Connie Chung is a journalist.

When Love is Newsworthy

Have you ever heard the saying, "Absence makes the heart grow fonder."? This couple has certainly proven this theory. They enjoyed a long distance, off again-on again courtship leading to marriage that took seven years. What makes the story interesting is that this couple's high-profile relationship has stood the test of time by using a rather unique strategy. That makes the love story of journalists Maury Povich and Connie Chung newsworthy.

Though they knew each other in 1969 when Maury was married and the co-star of Panorama, they became reacquainted in 1977 when they were paired as co-anchors on KNXT in LA. Working at this station was very stressful because it had low ratings. It did not end well for Maury. After six months, he was fired from the station and his first marriage ended. There was, however, a silver lining in this cloud—these events drew Connie and Maury closer, and they began to date.

Maury stayed in the California area for a couple of years and then headed back east. The two dated others but kept in touch. They missed each other and decided to resume their relationship, flying back and forth to see each other.

While they loved each other, both felt nervous about making the ultimate commitment. They never seemed to be ready at the same time. Finally, in 1984, they both found the courage to walk down the road of matrimony. Later, they adopted their son.

THE CHALLENGES

Their personalities are very different. Maury is outgoing while Connie is more reserved. Other stressors on their relationship included:

- The couple was unable to have children.
- For a while they had a long-distance marriage.
- They both had different interests.

Throughout all of this, they are still making headlines.

THE SECRETS OF THEIR SUCCESS

When asked what makes their relationship work, Maury and Connie agree that they don't do anything together. As unconventional as that sounds the pair insists that it works because it gives them the space they need to pursue their own interests. They also shared that being in the same business allowed them to be understanding of each other and to take pride in each other's accomplishments.

When they had a commuter marriage it was difficult but they survived it by racking up frequent-flyer miles. When they had difficulty conceiving a child, they adopted a son. By all accounts this couple is making it work for them.

The Moral of This Story

Love is appreciating your differences as well as your similarities.

ANONYMOUS

Notes

DonnaE!/Library of Congress

Abraham and Mary Todd Lincoln
Married: November 4, 1842

Abraham Lincoln was the 16th President of the United States. He signed the Emancipation Proclamation that freed slaves within the Confederacy in 1863. He was also married with four sons. Mary Todd Lincoln, Abe's wife, served as first lady during Lincoln's tenure as president.

When Opposites Attract

This couple is a textbook example of opposites attracting. When Honest Abe met Mary Todd he was 31 and she was 21. She came from a wealthy, politically-connected family. His family was poor and, at that time, he had no political prospects. Needless to say, her family was not impressed by Abe and was unsupportive of their relationship. Nonetheless, Mary (whose goal, among others, was to eventually be the First Lady) saw something they didn't see, fell in love, and accepted his marriage proposal. In early 1841, after an argument Abe broke their engagement. In the fall of 1842, however they resumed the relationship. They married on November fourth of that year. Having had no time to alert them of their plans, Mary's father and stepmother were not present.

THE CHALLENGES

Their differences did not stop at their ages and backgrounds. He was quiet, she was a talker. During arguments, Mary screamed and threw things. Abe walked away. He was thrifty and she liked to spend. Clearly, while they were *attracted* to each other, *living* with each other proved to be bit more work than they had anticipated.

Other stressors on the relationship:

- Mary was a staunch abolitionist even though her relatives served in the Confederate army and owned slaves. She was also accused of meddling in her husband's political appointments.
- The country was in the middle of the Civil War and constant death threats were being made against Abe.

- Abe had to travel a lot and Mary felt abandoned.
- Sometimes friends and family gave unsolicited advice. For example, Mary's sister Elizabeth Edwards had advised her not to marry Abe. When she did it anyway and problems arose, Elizabeth would take the opportunity to imply, "I told you so...."
- Three of their four sons died of diseases at early ages (only the eldest lived to adulthood).

Both of them, with good reason, were often depressed. To escape the misery, he threw himself into his work and she engaged in retail therapy. Her overspending eventually became a political problem for him.

Throughout all of this, they made it to the finish line.

THE SECRETS OF THEIR SUCCESS

While this political pair endured quite a lot of turmoil, it wasn't all tragic. Abe was President of the (somewhat) United States and Mary was the First Lady. She was a political junkie who gave him great insights. Mary was also a skilled conversationalist and an avid reader. She would read books and give Abe such detailed highlights that he would never have to read the book himself. They had the joy of bringing children into the world. Mary loved to dress up and be his "eye candy" and he loved to look at her. They had parties, went to plays and had great social standing. More importantly, they had each other. It was them against the world.

So much has been said and written about the Lincoln marriage but the following quotes indicate how the couple described their own feelings:

Abraham about Mary: "My wife is as handsome as when she was a girl and I, a poor nobody then, fell in love with her and what is more I have never fallen out."

Mary about Abraham: "Mr. Lincoln was the kindest man and most loving husband and father in the world."

Regardless of what others said, Mary knew that her decision to marry Abe worked for her and Abe absolutely adored her. They were both committed to their relationship.

The Moral of This Story

Opposites may attract, but it is the strength of their commitment that will keep them together.

DONNA M. N. EDWARDS

Notes

Keystone Pictures USA / Alamy stock Photos

David Jones and Iman
Married: April 24, 1992

David (Bowie) Jones was a rock star.
Iman is a super model and an entrepreneur.

When the Runway Meets the Stage

Two megastars were introduced at a dinner party. She was a supermodel and he was a rock star. Both had been previously married and each had a child. Could all that shine exist in one galaxy?

David openly admitted he fell hard for Iman the first time he saw her. He was so overwhelmed by his feelings that he said he began to mentally "name their children." Iman was not convinced that she was ready for a relationship with someone like him.

For their first date, he invited her to tea, even though he did not drink tea. Their relationship progressed from there and they never looked back. He was so taken with her, he would tie her shoes for her—a practice he continued during their marriage.

David proposed to Iman over the Seine River in Paris. She accepted and saw the ring she liked in Italy. By the time he located the ring, it had already been purchased. That did not deter the persistent and doting David. He bought it from the owner and presented it to Iman. In April 1992, they were married in Switzerland in a private ceremony and then again in Florence, Italy in June of the same year. They had one child together, Alexa and they remained married until David's death.

THE CHALLENGES

Though they were intensely guarded about their relationship, here are some of the known challenges:

- They had different backgrounds—she is Somalian and he was British.
- They were both major celebrities with healthy egos.

- They had to endure all the negative aspects of celebrity status (i.e., rumors about his sexuality, media glare, etc...).
- David was more of a homebody than she is.
- His illness was difficult for them both.

Yet their relationship remained the center of their universe.

THE SECRETS OF THEIR SUCCESS

Iman cited several things that led to the success of their marriage. She believes that timing played a crucial role because they were both in the right place to settle down. According to her, women often try to have it all at the same time. Her advice is when you are considering marriage, determine if you can make that your first priority. If not, don't get married. She believes that you can have it all but *not* at the same time.

Another factor that led to success in their marriage was that each left their egos at the door. They had to separate the person from the persona. Iman said it best when she said, "I fell in love with David Jones not David Bowie." This attitude transcended the difference in their backgrounds and all other barriers they had to face.

She also believes that you should do some things that are separate. She shared that while David was a musician and she was involved in her business ventures, their home life remained personal and separate. They did not respond or react to rumors and media gossip.

While his illness took a toll on them both, Iman was always there for him. They were always a team. David shared, "The greatest thing you will ever learn is to love and be loved in return."

The Moral of This Story

Excitement and fire are not qualities inherent to relation-ships. They are what happen when two people make marriage their number one priority.

Michele Weiner-Davis

Notes

Moviestore Collection Ltd / Alamy Stock Photos
Steve and Terri Irwin
Married: June 4, 1992

Steve Irwin was a nature expert and television personality, known for the show "Crocodile Hunter." Terri Irwin is an author, conservationist, and naturalist.

The Wildlife After the Wedding

On October 6, 1991, Terri a native of Eugene, Oregon, took a trip to Australia and visited a reptile park. It was there that she saw the man who, in less than a year from that date, would introduce her to the wilder side of life. Steve had just finished his crocodile show and Terri was impressed. She introduced herself and asked for a picture with him. They talked and knew they were soul mates. On February 2, 1992, when Terri returned to Australia they became engaged and by June they married. In lieu of a traditional honeymoon the couple opted to be filmed trapping crocodiles. This footage became the first segment on their *Crocodile Hunter* series. They co-starred on the show for five years. They had two children Bindi and Robert.

THE CHALLENGES

- Some accused Irwin of having a rather basic view of conservation in Australia and questioned his politics.
- The Irwin family was very transparent about their personal lives.
- In 2000, Steve's mother died unexpectedly.
- Steve was criticized for feeding crocodiles while holding his child.

Throughout all of it, they remained excited about their work
and each other until Steve's untimely death in 2006.

THE SECRETS OF THEIR SUCCESS

This marriage was a true partnership in every sense of the word. They were both passionate about animals and the environment. They were attracted to each other. Both were family oriented and they agreed on major issues. They not only had plans and vision, they stayed on message. They even seemed genuinely surprised that Steve drew the criticism of television viewers for feeding the crocodiles while holding their son. Both believed that Steve had the situation under control. When Steve's mother died (their birthdays were on the same day), he not only had to manage his own grief, he had to support his father who considered suicide. Terri was there to help them both.

While Terri marveled that Steve shared their most intimate moments on television (i.e., showing him delivering one of their children), she seemed to support him in doing so. They were reality stars before that term became popular. On September 4, 2006, Steve died after being pierced in the chest by a stingray during the taping of a show. It would have been interesting to see how their relationship might have evolved had he lived. How fortunate for them that even though they did not grow old together, they had the opportunity to live out their dreams.

The Moral of This Story

Don't marry the person you think you can live with; marry only the individual you think you can't live without.

JAMES DOBSON

Notes

Moviestore collection Ltd / Alamy Stock Photo

Gracie Allen and George Burns
Married: January 7, 1926

*Gracie Allen and George Burns were successful
comics who entertained film, radio, and
television audiences for over 35 years.*

When Love is a Laughing Matter

In the early 1920s as she went through the motions of secretarial school, Gracie Allen daydreamed about her big break in show business. Her roommate took her to a show and told her that the comedy team of George Burns and William Lorraine was splitting up and that William was in the market for a new partner. Gracie mistook George for William and she asked him about becoming a team. Several days later, George confessed his true identity, but Gracie still agreed to work with him.

The Burns and Allen partnership began with George writing the comedic sketches. George played the "jokester" and Gracie was the "straight" person. When George observed that the audience responded to the naturally comedic Gracie, but missed his jokes, he flipped the script. George rewrote their sketches to give her the punchlines and he became the straight man. This became their new routine and it was a hit.

While George's quick script change was successful on a professional level, his attempt to make a script change with Gracie on a personal level was not that simple. When Gracie went to work with George she was engaged to an entertainer named Benny Ryan. In 1925, she almost married Ryan, but had to wait because she had to complete a tour that was out of town. On that trip, Burns proposed to Allen; but she refused. Still he kept a ring in his pocket until she agreed to marry him. There are several stories as to how he convinced her to marry him:

Story 1
George presented her with an ultimatum: Either she married him or the act was finished. Gracie gave in.

Story 2
At a Christmas party, he accidentally made Gracie cry and she changed her mind about him. She felt that since he was the only boy who could make her cry, he must be "the one".
Story 3
Both Story 1 and Story 2 are accurate.

At any rate, in Ohio on January 7, 1926, they finally became man and wife. They adopted two children and enjoyed a long, successful partnership and an even longer, successful marriage.

THE CHALLENGES

George and Gracie's relationship was not all laughs. They had their share of struggles:

- They had different religious backgrounds. She was Irish Catholic and he was Jewish, the son of two Orthodox Jewish immigrants. While it was not a problem between the two of them, mixed religious marriages were considered very risky at that time.
- In the 1950s, George had one night of infidelity.
- Gracie was very insecure about her left arm and shoulder which had been disfigured as a result of a bad childhood burn.
- Gracie had health issues. She suffered from horrible migraine headaches and in the 1950s and 1960s had heart problems.

Through all of this, they persevered.

THE SECRETS OF THEIR SUCCESS

It is difficult to separate George and Gracie's professional and personal lives. Clearly the common denominator of both relationships was humor. The ever-self-effacing George was quick to give Gracie all the credit for their successes, in and out of the marriage. George wrote that, "I was a lousy lover. But Gracie married me for laughs, not for sex. Of course, she got both of them—when we had sex, she laughed."

When George briefly strayed, she gave him "grace." He noted that, "I was very lucky that Gracie handled it the way she did. My mistake could have ruined both our lives." Her ability to forgive and his commitment to remain faithful from then on saved their friendship and re-established their trust for one another.

This couple respected each other's talents. George once said, "She had the talent onstage and I had the talent offstage." They were able to maintain their symbiotic relationship even when George had to work alone because she was sick. Then Gracie died.

Though after Gracie's death George had difficulty adjusting, he enjoyed a successful solo night club and movie career. He visited her grave once a month for the rest of his life.

At the age of 100 George died—32 years after Gracie. He had pre-arranged for the marker on their gravesite to be changed upon his death. He instructed that it reflect what he had been looking forward to for over three decades: "Gracie Allen (1902–1964) and George Burns (1896–1996)—Together Again." As a final tribute to her, he insisted that Gracie's name be listed first to give her top billing.

The Moral of This Story

Sexiness wears thin after a while and beauty fades, but to be married to a man [or woman] who makes you laugh every day, ah, now that is a treat.

JOANNE WOODWARD (WIFE OF ACTOR PAUL NEWMAN)

Notes

Alalmy Stock Photo

Simone and James Todd Smith
Married: August 7, 1995

Simone is a philanthropist and entrepreneur.
James Todd Smith (LL Cool J) is an rapper,
actor, author, and entrepreneur.

Around the Way Love

E aster is one of the most significant holidays for Christians. It also holds a special place on this couple's timeline because it marks the beginning of their story. One Easter Sunday Todd was driving around his neighborhood and stopped at a friend's house. His friend offered to introduce him to his cousin. Todd was reluctant at first until he saw Cousin Simone. Not only was she cute, she had an attitude that Todd immortalized in his song, "Around the Way Girl." At that moment, unbeknownst to them, they had started the rest of their lives together.

Shortly after that initial meeting, they began to date, but then Todd had to go on tour for eight weeks. At his request, Simone agreed not to date anyone else. She understood how serious he was when at a Miami concert he brought her on stage and serenaded her with his song "I Need Love." Then, in front of the entire audience, he kissed her. GAME OVER.

There were still some issues they had to iron out so they dated off and on for about eight years. Then one day, Todd proposed to her while they were taking a ride in his Porsche. According to him, he sped and would not slow down until she agreed. They have four children together and still live in love's fast lane.

THE CHALLENGES

Marriage is a game changer – especially when one or both of the partners are in the limelight. Let's be honest, there can't be light without shade and every couple experiences some of both. Some of Todd and Simone's tougher moments include:

- In the music industry sexuality often becomes part of the act. Simone was not comfortable with the way Todd's sexuality was expressed in the video "Doin' It."

- In 2004, Simone was diagnosed with a rare type of cancer. Her rehabilitation took over two years and Todd and the entire family had to put their full efforts into supporting her.
- Their son was involved in a minor incident in a New York club. Frequently children who have mega star parents are seen as spoiled and privileged. Rarely do people understand the unforgiving fish bowl existence they are forced to navigate. Unlike most of us who are allowed to make our mistakes in anonymity, children of mega stars are often not afforded that luxury.

THE SECRETS OF THEIR SUCCESS

While Todd and Simone got married in 1995, they have been together since 1987. His advice on maintaining a happy marriage is to, "Be friends, keep it simple, know what to overlook, and be quiet, eat my soup, and let her talk." He also mentioned that he stays in shape, puts his family before his career, tries to consistently support his wife, and strives to resolve issues rather than win arguments.

With regard to Simone's displeasure with the video "Doing It", the couple had to negotiate what appropriate boundaries would look like in the future. What is also significant is that she did not allow the issue to become more important to her than loving Todd.

Simone shares that she puts God in the forefront of everything and prays often. This helps put everything in perspective, even the media glare. Simone agrees with Todd that their marriage and family come first. She believes in compromising with a win-win outcome in mind. Simone also advises that you pick your battles and make quality time for your spouse.

The Moral of This Story

Never let a problem to be solved become more important than a person to be loved.

BARBARA JOHNSON

Notes

WENN Ltd / Alamy Stock Photos

Marco and Jeanette Rubio
Married: October 17, 1998

Marco Rubio has been a U. S. Republican
Senator from Florida since 2011.
Jeanette is a housewife, a philanthropist, and a volunteer.

Speaker of Their House

They were both from the same neighborhood and had attended the same high school. In 1990, outgoing Marco who was 19 and in college, met bashful Jeanette who was 17 and in high school. This led to a movie date and a lengthy courtship. When Marco was attending the University of Florida the two kept in contact and, for a time, corresponded in writing. She worked and was briefly an NFL cheerleader. Then their relationship became a casualty of distance and they broke it off.

During their separation, Marco tried to enjoy the Miami club scene. It wasn't long before he recognized where he really wanted to be. He walked to the nearest phone booth and dialed the ten-digit phone number of the woman who would help shape his destiny.

This time when Marco and Jeanette reconnected, she became his priority. On Valentine's Day in 1997, he proposed to her on the top of the Empire State Building, simulating a scene from one of her favorite movies "Sleepless in Seattle." Marco and Jeanette married in 1998 and now have four children.

Then Marco entered the Twilight Zone
(otherwise known as politics).

THE CHALLENGES

Marco's political involvement brought about the usual onslaught of unwanted attention. Any of the couple's personal weaknesses become fodder for the press. There were also ordinary relationship issues that had to be addressed such as:

- He is an extrovert and she is an introvert.
- Marco was away from the home for significant periods of time.
- Her career was not as vibrant as his.

Throughout all of this, they have elected to stay together.

THE SECRETS OF THEIR SUCCESS

This union is successful because they work at it. While they are not perfect, they are intentional about balancing their public and personal lives. On a personal level, Marco and Jeanette have identified support systems to help them stay connected in a meaningful way. They have active spiritual lives, attend couples retreats, and engage in honest and open conversation. When Jeanette felt that they needed more time in their personal lives she shared that with Marco. This led her to charge his staff with arranging his travel schedule such that it would bring him home at night whenever humanly possible. She is also known to visit him in Tallahassee, where he works, to remind him of his family responsibilities.

As Marco's political career advanced and he became a Senator, Jeanette's priorities shifted and she became the Speaker of *Their* House. Rather than pursuing a separate career outside of the home, she focuses on family and bringing issues she feels passionate about to Marco's platform. She has become the moral compass for their family. Amidst all the public noise, they know that the most important conversations occur with God, their family, and each other. No matter what goes on, they pay attention and stay on message.

The Moral of This Story

Love is not about grand intentions. It is about small attentions.

ROBERT BRAULT

Notes

DonnaE!/Depositphotos.com

Tammy and Kirk Franklin
Married: January 20, 1996

Tammy Franklin is a housewife and philanthropist.
Kirk Dewayne Franklin is a Grammy Award winning
American gospel musician, choir director, and author.

Mark 19:6 "...Therefore What God Has Joined, Let No One Separate..."

When he was eighteen, Kirk met Tammy at a swim party and was completely taken with her. He even proposed to her. She did not accept immediately. For a while they had a long-distance relationship and were even separated for three years.

Then they both thought long and hard and decided they would marry. Kirk had a child from another relationship and so did she. Once they married, Kirk adopted her child. They went on to have two children together. They may be a match made in heaven but some of their experiences were well south of that border.

THE CHALLENGES

Kirk and Tammy had very different backgrounds. She was raised in a large two parent family and he was raised by an elderly aunt. Other stressors in their relationship included:

- Kirk was once addicted to pornography.
- Tammy had to learn to listen to Kirk's concerns without trying to solve all of his problems.
- Tammy was home alone with the children because of Kirk's busy schedule.
- Kirk was badly injured as a result of a nine-foot fall into an orchestra pit.
- Tammy's concern with transitioning from a mother of minors to a mother of young adults.

Through all of this, God preserved their resolve.

THE SECRETS OF THEIR SUCCESS

Kirk insists that to have a successful marriage, divorce must take place. He recommends that people divorce their bad habits to be what Christ intended in their lives, overall as well as in your marriage. He had to divorce his bad habits one of which was watching pornography. His wife forgave him, they prayed together and she helped him through his recovery.

Another habit he had to divorce was pushing people away before they could leave him. Again, Tammy forgave him and waited for him to mature. According to Kirk, Tammy was more patient than she should have been with him, but he is grateful for it. After he fell and was hospitalized, Tammy stayed by his side and supported him through his physical healing.

When Tammy needed support, Kirk was there for her. She, like many mothers, was feeling at a loss when her children left home. She didn't have a plan for her life after raising minor children. It was Kirk who encouraged her to dream beyond their family.

Tammy recommends an active prayer life to sustain marriage and family. Although her husband travels frequently, she feels their marriage has a divine purpose and that God wants it to be an example for others.

Kirk praised his wife for upholding her standards and not criticizing him as he experienced his trials. He shared that she is the inspiration for his lyrics. Kirk explained that while their marriage isn't perfect, they struggle together.

One final bit of wisdom Tammy gave is, "… I've learned … that truly being a good wife is listening to my husband's needs, dreams, and even at times, his need to vent and for me to simply listen and not try to fix it. And above all, say a lil' prayer." AMEN.

The Moral of This Story

Above all, love each other deeply, because love covers a multitude of sins.

1 PETER 4:8

Notes

Richard Ellis / Alamy Stock Photo
James Carville and Mary Matalin
Married: November 25, 1993

James Carville is an American political commentator and media personality who is a prominent figure in the Democratic Party. Mary Matalin is an American political consultant well known for her work with the Republican Party.

When Love is Politically Incorrect

What are the odds that Mary, a South Side of Chicago native and staunch Republican would fall in love with James, a rural Louisiana native and an unapologetic Democrat? Believe it or not, this long shot actually paid off.

They met in 1991 and later began dating. Their dates ranged from dinner parties with political consultants to having vodka and French fries. Mary confessed that she was "struck, stayed struck, and am struck."

By 1992, Mary was the deputy director for President George H.W. Bush's re-election campaign and James was the key strategist for Bush's opponent Bill Clinton. They pushed the pause button on their relationship until the campaign was over. Ultimately, Clinton won easily and Mary was depressed. James, on the other hand, became a rising star of the Democratic Party. Still, they resumed their relationship. Mary explained that it was hard to lose but that she "stayed in love instead of in darkness." Apparently, James also stayed in love because on Thanksgiving Day 1993, he and Mary married. They have much to be thankful for as they are still together and have two daughters, Emmy and Matty.

CHALLENGES

As you might imagine, this couple experienced their fair share of issues to debate:

- The couple have opposing political views.
- Mary had feelings of detachment from James (he seemed impatient and hyperactive).
- They sometimes disagreed on how to handle finances.

Yet, they are still crazy (about each other) after all these years.

THE SECRETS OF THEIR SUCCESS

Mary explained they are not a democracy but an enlightened MOM-archy. She feels that the success of their marriage is based on faith, family and good wine. James' viewpoint is that he does not have a position on anything domestically. He maintains that in order to have a successful marriage he surrenders, capitulates, and retreats. There is one hard and fast rule that they both adhere to—they do not discuss politics in their home.

Incidentally, those feelings of detachment Mary felt were not imagined. James was diagnosed with ADHD (Attention Deficit Hyperactivity Disorder) and impatience and hyperactivity are symptoms of that disorder. It is also common for loved ones to feel detached from the affected individual. The diagnosis helped to clarify his behavior and intentions, and made a positive impact on their future interactions.

Notwithstanding their differences, the couple has managed to collaborate on at least two best seller list books. James proudly admits that he enjoys having the smartest and prettiest wife in town. Mary says that what she loves about him the most is that "he loves us." James gave this simple and honest assessment of their relationship when he said, "I ... think that at the end of the day, it's one of those kind of unexplainable things."

The Moral of This Story

The goal of marriage is not to think alike but to think together.

Robert C. Dodds

Notes

Epilogue

*"Marriage is not supposed to be easy—
it's supposed to be worth it."*

At a time when the institution of a marriage has been criticized and questioned, people wonder if it is worth it. I find it addictive to celebrate those couples who continue to prove that it is.

Though these celebrity marriages were very different from one another, they shared one common element. The couples not only believed their love was worth more than any problems they had, *they acted on that belief.* They had risen to the occasion during the defining moments of their relationships when they had suffered the toughest setbacks.

In sustained marriages, this dynamic is common. My husband and I were in the midst of putting a second-floor addition on our house when the aftermath of a tropical storm swept through our region. It ruined nearly all of our furniture and damaged the hardwood floors. I cried. He grumbled in anger. Then we prayed and thanked God no one was hurt. Eventually, we completed the job. It was tough financially and emotionally, but we got through it.

The Wedlock Chronicles, Volume 1 is evidence that it *is* possible for the benefits of marriage to far outweigh the deficits. This written journey has brought me full circle—hopeful that our daughter and her fiancé will find their experience worth it.

Index of Quotes

for reflection

"It is better to lose your pride with someone you love rather than to lose that someone you love with your useless pride." *John Ruskin*   29

"Lean on each other's strengths and forgive each other's weaknesses." *Anonymous*   24

"Long-lasting love doesn't happen by accident - ... Love is deliberate, it's intentional, it's purposeful, and in the end, it's worth every minute that we give of ourselves to another." *Darlene Schacht*   56

"Love is a partnership of two unique people who bring out the very best in each other, and who know that even though they are wonderful as individuals, they are even better together." *Barbara Cage*   69

"Love is appreciating your differences as well as your similarities." *Anonymous*   73

"Love is not about grand intentions. It is about small attentions." *Robert Brault*   99

"Love me when I least deserve it because that is when I really need it." *Swedish Proverb*   34

"Marriages are at their best when the husband and the wife demonstrate that they are on the same side." *Anonymous*   3

"Never let a problem to be solved become more important than a person to be loved." *Barbara Johnson*   95

"Opposites may attract, but it is the strength of their
commitment that will keep them together." *Donna M. N. Edwards*   78

"Personal worth is not negotiable and commitments, not promises,
sustain a relationship." *Donna M. N. Edwards*   43

"Sexiness wears thin after a while and beauty fades, but to be
married to a man [or woman] who makes you laugh every day,
ah, now that is a treat."
Joanne Woodward (wife of actor Paul Newman)   91

"The goal of marriage is not to think alike but to think together."
Robert C. Dodds   107

"The success of marriage comes not in finding the "right" person,
but in the ability of both partners to adjust to the real person
they inevitably realize they married." *John Fischer*   38

"You have to do the work in your marriage, but it has to be
laid on a strong foundation of love." *Robin Wright*   20

About the Author

Donna M. N. Edwards is a retired sociologist and school administrator. A wife for over thirty years, Edwards has two adult children and lives with her husband in Washington, DC.

74615553R00072

Made in the USA
Columbia, SC
03 August 2017